HOW DID WE FIND OUT

ABOUT VOLCANOES?

HOW DID WE FIND OUT . . . SERIES
Each of the books in this series on the history of
science emphasizes the process of discovery.

How Did We Find Out . . . ?
Books by Isaac Asimov

HOW DID WE FIND OUT THE EARTH IS ROUND?

HOW DID WE FIND OUT ABOUT ELECTRICITY?

HOW DID WE FIND OUT ABOUT NUMBERS?

HOW DID WE FIND OUT ABOUT DINOSAURS?

HOW DID WE FIND OUT ABOUT GERMS?

HOW DID WE FIND OUT ABOUT VITAMINS?

HOW DID WE FIND OUT ABOUT COMETS?

HOW DID WE FIND OUT ABOUT ENERGY?

HOW DID WE FIND OUT ABOUT ATOMS?

HOW DID WE FIND OUT ABOUT NUCLEAR POWER?

HOW DID WE FIND OUT ABOUT OUTER SPACE?

HOW DID WE FIND OUT ABOUT EARTHQUAKES?

HOW DID WE FIND OUT ABOUT BLACK HOLES?

HOW DID WE FIND OUT ABOUT OUR HUMAN ROOTS?

HOW DID WE FIND OUT ABOUT ANTARCTICA?

HOW DID WE FIND OUT ABOUT OIL?

HOW DID WE FIND OUT ABOUT COAL?

HOW DID WE FIND OUT ABOUT SOLAR POWER?

HOW DID WE FIND OUT ABOUT VOLCANOES?

HOW DID WE FIND OUT

ABOUT VOLCANOES?

Isaac Asimov
Illustrated by David Wool

WALKER AND COMPANY
New York

1981

Library of Congress Cataloging in Publication Data

Asimov, Isaac, 1920–
  How did we find out about volcanoes?

  Includes index.
  Summary: Discusses the features of a
volcano, the causes of eruptions, and the
locations of active volcanoes on earth and
elsewhere in our solar system.
  1. Volcanoes—Juvenile literature.
[1. Volcanoes] I. Wool, David. II. Title.
QE521.3.A84 1981   551.2′1   80-54394
ISBN 0-8027-6411-8   AACR2
ISBN 0-8027-6412-6 (lib. bdg.)

First published in the United States of America
in 1981 by the Walker Publishing Company, Inc.

Published simultaneously in Canada by Beaverbooks,
Limited, Don Mills, Ontario.

Trade ISBN: 0-8027-6411-8
Reinf. ISBN: 0-8027-6412-6

Library of Congress Catalog Card Number: 80-54394

Printed in the United States of America

10 9 8 7 6 5 4 3 2 1

To
Jesse and Rochelle Shereff
and that delicious cheesecake.

Contents

1   Explosion at Thera   9

2   Ancient Thoughts About Volcanoes   19

3   Great Volcanic Eruptions   26

4   The Heat Below Our Feet   47

5   Volcanoes on Other Worlds   57

    Index   63

FRAGMENT OF FRESCO FROM CRETE

1 Explosion at Thera

IN EUROPE, civilization first developed on the islands of the Aegean Sea (ee-JEE-an), which lies between the modern nations of Greece and Turkey.

The largest island of the area is Crete (KREET). It is 3,189 square miles in size, or as large as Rhode Island and Delaware put together. As early as 3000 B.C., Crete began to use metals and to develop an important culture.

Crete may have borrowed much from nearby lands that had an even older history. One such land was Egypt, four hundred miles southeast of Crete. Other lands were what is now known as Lebanon, Syria, and Iraq, six hundred miles to the east.

The older civilizations were on continents, on great tracts of land. Crete represented the first island civilization. It was interested in the sea, therefore, and was the first land to develop a navy. The Cretan ships protected the land from invasion, and the Cretan people lived comfortable and peaceful lives. They built large palaces

9

with indoor plumbing, created beautiful art, and played interesting athletic games.

The Cretan ships also traded with the surrounding lands. With the trade, the ships carried Cretan civilization and its way of life to other islands nearby and even to the part of the European continent we now call Greece.

About a hundred miles north of Crete are a group of islands known as the Cyclades (SIK-

AEGEAN SEA

luh-deez). This comes from a Greek word meaning "circle" because the chief islands of the group are arranged in a circle, more or less. Cretan civilization reached the Cyclades and the people of those small islands also grew prosperous.

The southernmost island of the Cyclades was called Thera (THEER-uh) by the ancient Greeks, though it is spelled Thira today. Italians controlled the Aegean Sea in the Middle Ages, and they called the island Santorini (san-tuh-REE-nee), a name which is still sometimes used today.

0   1   2 MILES

N

THERA TODAY

Thera is only sixty-five miles north of Crete. Many Cretan ships came to Thera and, beginning about 2000 B.C., Thera became a rich, civilized island and stayed so for five hundred years.

If you look at the map of Thera now, you will see that it is shaped like a half-circle with the opening to the west. It is only about 30 square miles in area, not much larger than the island of Manhattan.

In the opening between the top and bottom points of the half-circle are two small islands. It is almost as though Thera were originally a complete circle, like the letter O, but somehow the sea broke in from the west, leaving that part of the circle in pieces. In the center of the broken O are two tiny islands that constantly smoke as though there were fires under them.

Beginning in 1966 scientists, digging carefully at certain sites in Thera, found the ruins of the ancient city that was so wealthy and civilized in Cretan times. They found beautiful pottery and wall paintings.

They also found evidence of a violent explosion that must have taken place about 1500 B.C.

Thera, it seems, was actually a large mountain at that time, rising up from the bottom of the Aegean Sea. The top part, which was above the surface of the sea, was circular, so that the island was then a solid O.

It was not an ordinary mountain, however. Deep within it, there was great heat that was sometimes pushed up and sometimes sank down. Occasionally in mountains of this sort, as the heat

CRETAN WALL PAINTING

grows more intense, the rock inside the mountain melts. As more and more melting takes place, the melted rock comes closer and closer to the surface. Eventually, the heat can actually melt a hole somewhere in the mountain, and through that hole, red-hot, liquid rock can overflow and pour down the mountainside.

Such molten rock is called *lava* (LAH-vuh). This is from an Italian word meaning "to wash." Originally, the people of the Italian city of Naples used the word for a downpour of rain that washed the streets clean. It came to be applied to the overflowing stream of melted rock because it washed the side of the mountain clean of grass and trees.

The overflow of lava could be dangerous, of course. If there are houses and towns on the slopes and at the foot of the mountain, they can be destroyed and people can be killed.

Sometimes, more happens than just lava overflowing and pouring downward. If water seeps deep into the mountain, the growing heat will make it boil. The steam produces more and more pressure, and finally it can blow out a piece of the mountain with great force.

This is an *eruption* (ee-RUP-shun) from Latin words meaning "to explode." Great rocks are hurled high in the air. Clouds of ash and gas are thrown to great heights. Columns of fire arise and lava pours out in great quantities.

Some mountains of this sort are always smoking and heating. But every once in a while it gets a little worse and the lava flows. Such mountains are not usually very dangerous. As long as they keep overflowing now and then, they are not likely to explode. Also, people know that it is uncomfortable to get too close to it, and they stay away and remain safe.

On the other hand, some mountains of this sort are quiet for many centuries. People forget it ever produced lava and think of it as just another mountain. The old lava that once poured out of it makes very fertile soil, so that plants grow on the slopes of the mountain and make it look green and pleasant. People find that crops grow well there, so they establish farms and homes on the slopes and at the foot of the mountain. Pretty soon towns grow up.

Then, someday, the mountain begins to heat up again, and if steam begins to form far in the depth,

DESTRUCTION OF THERA

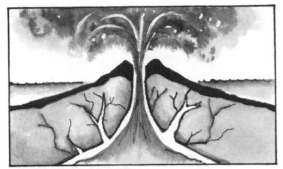

1. ERUPTION OF LAVA

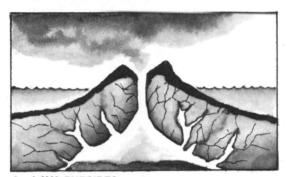

2. LAVA SUBSIDES
   SEA WATER SEEPS IN AND EXPLODES

3. ISLAND COLLAPSES ON ITSELF

it is held in by a great weight of rock that cooled down centuries before. The pressure builds up—and builds up—and builds up—

It builds up much higher than it would have if the mountain hadn't been quiet for so long and hadn't developed such a thick layer of lava that had cooled into solid rock. Finally there's an *enormous* explosion.

In 1500 B.C. the mountain on Thera exploded. It blew up and scattered itself into the upper air in a vast cloud of rocks and dust and ash. A big hole was left where it stood. The sea rushed into the hole, and the island, instead of being a solid round circle of land, became a broken ring.

Everyone on the island was surely killed, and ash and dust showered down on eastern Crete.

The bottom of the sea shook and that set up a large wave. Some people call this a tidal wave, but it has nothing to do with tides. A better name is *tsunami* (tsoo-NAH-mee), which is Japanese for "harbor waves." When such a wave, which is quite low in the open sea, enters a harbor, all the water is forced into a narrow place and it becomes very high. It can be fifty feet high or more and when it crashes onto the shore, it can drown thousands of people.

The shores of Crete and of Greece were battered by the tsunami. Crete's capital city of Knossos (NOSS-us) was badly damaged, and the whole island suffered a great disaster.

The people of Crete tried to carry on after this dreadful blow, but they could not recover. Fifty years later, about 1450 B.C., invaders from Greece

PLATO

conquered the island, burned its cities, and de-
• stroyed its civilization. It might not have happened, had it not been for that exploding mountain on Thera.

The later Greeks had a dim memory of that
huge explosion. They had a legend about a great
flood that swept over the land, a flood from which
only one couple escaped. This could be a tale
about the tsunami that once had struck Greece.

About 370 B.C., the Greek philosopher, Plato
(PLAY-toh), 427–347 B.C.) wrote of a great and
beautiful city that was destroyed overnight by an
earthquake and sank beneath the sea. He said it
was far to the west, in the ocean beyond Spain,
and he called it Atlantis (at-LAN-tis) after the
name of the Atlantic Ocean, in which he had located it.

For over two thousand years, people have won-
dered if there was something to the legend. Many
people actually believed that somewhere beneath
the waters of the Atlantic Ocean there was a
drowned continent that had once been a great
civilized nation.

Possibly, though, Plato was repeating something that was a memory of an event closer to
home. The story may have originated with the
island of Thera, which had been highly civilized
but which had exploded and sunk beneath the
sea.

2 Ancient Thoughts About Volcanoes

THERA IS NOT the only case of a mountain from which smoke and lava issued.

There are small islands just north of the large Mediterranean island of Sicily (SIH-sih-lee). They are the Lipari Islands (LIP-uh-ree), and, like Thera, they are really mountains made up of cooled lava built up from the sea bottom.

The southernmost of the Lipari Islands is named Vulcano (vool-KAHN-oh), and its mountain is always glowing and smoking. Like other such mountains, it has a cup-shaped depression near the top. Such a depression is called a crater (KRAY-ter), from the Latin word for "cup." Sometimes lava wells up into the crater and over the lip to pour down the mountain slope. The last time there was an active eruption of this sort on Mount Vulcano was in 1890.

For some reason the ancient Italian people, including the early Romans, were impressed by this particular island. The god of fire was important in the early legends of many people, and the ancient Italians called this god Vulcan (VUL-kan). No one

STROMBOLI VOLCANO IN THE LIPARI ISLANDS

can be sure whether the god was named for the island with the fiery mountain on it or whether the island was named for the god.

In later times the Romans decided that Vulcan was identical with the Greek god Hephaestus (huh-FES-tus), the god of the forge, where he made things out of heated metal. Hephaestus or Vulcan was often pictured as laboring over a hot fire as a smith god, forming beautiful ornaments and tools out of gold, silver, copper, bronze, and iron.

It seemed natural to suppose that the god's forge was located inside some hot and smoking mountain, perhaps the one on the island of Vulcano. The heat and smoke were thought to come out of the work at Vulcan's forge. When the work grew too active and Vulcan himself perhaps got too excited, then the fire of the forge got out of hand, melted the rock, and lava poured out of the crater.

The name of Vulcan and his island became attached to all mountains of this sort. To this day we call them *volcanoes* (vol-KAY-noze).

It isn't the least bit surprising that ancient people thought that supernatural beings were inside volcanoes. The heat and lava and the earthquakes that almost always accompanied the eruptions could to them only be the result of godlike power.

Even the ancient Israelites felt awed by volcanoes. Thus, the Bible describes how, after the Israelites left Egypt, they came to Mount Sinai (SIGH-nigh), where Moses obtained the Law from God. The Bible says, "on the third day of the morning . . . there were thunders and lightnings, and a thick cloud upon the mount. . . . And Mount Sinai was altogether on a smoke . . . and the whole mount quaked greatly."

We can't tell exactly where Mount Sinai was from the Biblical description, but perhaps it was a volcanic mountain, and the early Israelites felt that the majesty of the Lord must dwell there.

The supernatural beings associated with volcanoes were not necessarily kindly gods or majestic lords of creation. Sometimes they were evil beings, awesome and frightening.

The tallest and most active volcano known to the ancient Greeks was Mount Etna (ET-nuh) in northeastern Sicily. It is about forty-five miles south of Mount Vulcano and is just over two miles high. Since the days of ancient Greece Mount Etna has erupted about 140 times, the last time in 1971.

Some ancients explained the activity of Mount Etna by tales of giants—monstrous creatures who fought against Zeus and the other gods. One of the giants was Enceladus (en-SEL-uh-dus). He was the largest and most ferocious of them. The goddess Athena (uh-THEE-nuh) beat him down by hurling a huge rock at him. The rock buried him and, in so doing, flattened out into the island of Sicily. Enceladus was forever imprisoned under the huge weight of the island and the exact spot under which he lay was Mount Etna. Since he was immortal, he lived on, and when he groaned, the mountain rumbled. When he stirred himself wrathfully in his attempts to escape, the lava overflowed and earthquakes shook the ground.

The more scientific thinkers among the ancient Greeks didn't really suppose that there were gods or giants under the volcanoes. They looked for more reasonable causes.

The philosopher Aristotle (AR-is-TOT-ul), 384–322 B.C.) thought there were regions of air imprisoned under the crust of the earth. These were hot and were constantly attempting to find

their way out of the depths. Sometimes such air would burst from one underground chamber into another, setting up vibrations that would make themselves felt as earthquakes, while their heat caused lava to overflow from a volcano.

A Greek geographer, Strabo (STRAY-boh, 63 B.C.–A.D. 19), agreed with Aristotle on this. He thought the volcanoes were safety valves that let the heat escape so that the air under the earth would quiet down. Without the chance for such an escape, the violent air might disrupt the earth altogether.

MT. ETNA

Whether there were hot collections of air underneath the crust might have seemed doubtful, but there could be no question about there being heat of some sort under the earth's crust. Unless there was, volcanoes could not be explained at all.

In fact, the sight of volcanoes made people certain that there was a very hot region under the surface of the earth. The notion grew that below the surface there was a region of fire, in which all those who rebelled against the gods were punished.

The ancient Greeks felt that the spirits of the dead lived in a shadowy kingdom called Hades (HAY-deez) far to the west, near the Atlantic Ocean. There they lived drearily, but they suffered no punishment. Far under the earth, however, the Greeks thought there was a place they called Tartarus (TAHR-tur-us), where great evildoers were endlessly punished in various ways.

The ancient Israelites felt the spirits of the dead lived underground in Sheol (SHEE-ole), which was much like the Greek Hades. As time went on, though, the later Jews became more familiar with Greek thought, and Sheol became more like Tartarus. It became what we today call Hell.

By New Testament times Hell was thought to be like the inside of a huge volcano.

Volcanoes send out streams of lava, which glow with heat, looking as though it is all on fire. Then, too, volcanoes send out clouds of gases formed from material deep underground. There is steam and carbon dioxide in great quantities, but these don't have an odor and aren't particularly noticeable. There is sulfur underground, however, and it burns and combines with oxygen to form a gas called *sulfur dioxide* (SUL-fur-digh-OK-side), which has a strong, choking smell.

An older name for sulfur is "brimstone," so sulfur dioxide is sometimes referred to as "the smell of brimstone."

For this reason brimstone is associated with volcanoes. Thus the Bible describes the destruction of the wicked cities of Sodom and Gomorrah; "Then the Lord rained upon Sodom and upon Gomorrah brimstone and fire."

It may be that the story of Sodom and Gomorrah represents a dim memory of cities destroyed by a volcanic eruption.

And because Hell is pictured as the inside of a volcano, it came to be thought that Hell was a place of "fire and brimstone." For that reason, preachers who threaten the people in the audience with Hell if they continue to sin are said to preach "fire and brimstone."

It all goes back to volcanoes.

3 Great Volcanic Eruptions

THE ANCIENT GREEKS and Romans didn't really understand how dangerous volcanoes might be. They knew that Mount Etna, Mount Vulcano, and a few others were always smoking and flashing and had to be watched. They did not quite realize that an apparently harmless mountain might suddenly explode and that whole cities might be wiped out in a short time.

There was the case of Thera, of course, but that had long been forgotten except for the legend of Atlantis, and that legend spoke only of an earthquake and not a volcano.

In the time of the early Roman Empire, however, there was a new and frightening example of what a volcanic eruption could do.

About fifteen miles east of the important city of Naples in southern Italy, there is a mountain called Vesuvius (vuh-SOO-vee-us). It is less than a mile high, and in ancient Roman times was considered just an ordinary mountain.

The Romans knew no writings of the past that mentioned smoke or ashes coming out of Vesu-

27

vius. The soil about it was fertile and there were many farms near it. On the southern slope of the mountain were two towns: Pompeii (pom-PAY) and Herculaneum (HUR-kyuh-LAY-nee-um).

Pompeii had been founded about 500 B.C., and for nearly six hundred years it had prospered. In the time of the early Roman emperors many rich Romans had villas there.

There were occasional earthquakes near Vesuvius to be sure, but there are earthquakes occasionally throughout the Mediterranean area. There was a pretty bad one in A.D. 63, during the time of the Emperor Nero. This shook the Roman cities quite a bit, but the people repaired the damage and went on as before.

In A.D. 79 there were several more small earthquakes, and then, on August 24, Vesuvius exploded. Clouds of ash, smoke, steam, and choking gas blanketed the whole mountain, and streams of lava flowed in the direction of Pompeii and Herculaneum. The townspeople, not understanding the danger, remained in town during the first stages of the eruption. When they decided it was time to get away, it was too late. Perhaps twenty thousand people died.

One of those who died was a well-known Roman writer usually known to us as Pliny (PLIH-nee, A.D. 23–79). He was on a ship in the nearby bay. Seeing Vesuvius smoking and erupting, he had himself put on shore in order to observe what was happening more closely. He was overcome by the fumes and died. The event was described in a report written by Pliny's nephew, Pliny the Younger (A.D. 62–113).

THE ERUPTION OF MT. VESUVIUS

Vesuvius never settled down completely after that. It would sometimes be fairly quiet for a couple of centuries, but then it would erupt again. In 1631 there was a particularly bad eruption, the worst since A.D. 79, and it killed about four thousand people. Since then quiet periods have rarely lasted for longer than ten years or so.

In 1709 people began to dig through the covering of soil and ash to expose what was left of the buildings of Pompeii. (Herculaneum is buried too deeply under solid lava to be uncovered easily.) What has been uncovered in Pompeii has told historians a great deal about how people lived in the time of the early Roman Empire. Such information could not have been obtained in any other way.

The ruins of Pompeii became a popular tourist attraction. Some of the uncovered material was on

THE RUINS OF POMPEII

display in New York in 1979 to mark the nineteen-hundredth anniversary of the eruption of Vesuvius.

Vesuvius is the only active volcano on the continent of Europe, but, of course, Mount Etna, on the island of Sicily, is larger and more dangerous. Mount Etna erupts frequently, and a particularly bad eruption in 1669 destroyed up to fourteen towns and killed up to twenty thousand people.

Some think that if all the eruptions of Mount

Etna are considered, perhaps as many as a million people have been killed by the volcano. Mount Etna is known to be a volcano, however, and everyone expects trouble and watches out for it. Vesuvius, on the other hand, caught everyone completely by surprise. It was that dramatic surprise that made Vesuvius's destruction of Pompeii and Herculaneum the most famous volcanic event in ancient times.

As the centuries passed, Europeans learned

more and more about the world and discovered there were dangerous volcanoes outside their own continent.

Consider Iceland, for instance. It lies five hundred miles northwest of Scotland and is as large as the state of Kentucky. It is far to the north, however—a cold land, with much of its area covered by ice. Despite that, it is also full of volcanoes, for there seems to be a lot of heat under the surface.

One of the volcanoes is Laki (LAH-kee) in south-central Iceland. In 1783 it began to erupt. For two years lava poured out of the crater, sometimes rapidly, sometimes slowly, until finally it covered 220 square miles.

The lava itself didn't do much damage, for there were not very many people in the area. However, Laki kept spewing out ash and sulfur dioxide fumes. The ash spread far and wide, falling over much of the island and some of it even reached Scotland.

The ash darkened the sky so that the crops, unable to get sunlight, died. The sulfur dioxide fumes killed three quarters of the domestic animals on the island. With crops gone and animals dead, ten thousand Icelanders, one fifth of the whole population of the island, died of starvation or disease.

Even worse volcanic eruptions took place in Indonesia (IN-doh-NEE-zhuh), a group of large islands off southeastern Asia. On Sumbawa (soom-BAH-wuh), a small island east of the big island of Java (JAV-uh), there is Mount Tambora (TAM-buh-ruh). This thirteen thousand-foot-high

VOLCANO IN ICELAND

volcano exploded on April 7, 1815, in the worst eruption the earth had seen since Thera.

The top four thousand feet of the mountain were blown off and about thirty-six cubic miles of rock and dust were hurled into the air. The rain of rock and dust killed twelve thousand people, and the destruction of farmland and domestic animals led to the death by starvation of eighty thousand more on Sumbawa and on the island of Lombok (LOM-bok) to its west.

Some of the huge quantity of rock and dust blown into the air reached a height of many miles and floated about in the upper air for months. The fine particles in the upper air reflected sunlight and allowed less of it to reach the ground. For that reason the temperatures on earth were lower than usual for a year or so.

In New England, for instance, 1816 was unusually cold, and there were freezing spells in every month of that year, even July and August. It was called the year without a summer. At the time the people of New England didn't know that they were having trouble because a volcano had blown its top on the other side of the world.

An even worse explosion occurred in Indonesia sixty-eight years later on Krakatoa (KRAK-uh-TOH-uh), a small island not quite as large as Manhattan, lying between the large islands of Java and Sumatra.

The whole island is a volcano, just as Thera was, but Mount Krakatoa didn't seem particularly dangerous. There had been a small eruption in 1680 and then nothing at all for two centuries.

Then, at 10 A.M. on August 27, 1883, the heat and pressure deep within had quietly built up to the point where the hardened lava in the volcano could no longer hold it back—and Krakatoa exploded!

It didn't send as much rock and dust into the sky as Mount Tambora had, but what it did send was sent with much more force. The noise of that explosion was unbelievably loud. It could be heard for thousands of miles in every direction. If Krakatoa had exploded in Kansas, everyone in the United States would have heard the noise, and so would many people in Canada and Mexico.

Volcanic rock and dust fell over an area of 300,000 square miles, an area larger than all of Texas. The explosion set up a vibration in the sea all round the small island, and a tsunami hit the nearby coasts of Sumatra and Java with waves of water up to 120 feet high. As a result, 163 villages were destroyed and nearly forty thousand people were killed.

The smaller quantity of ash in the upper atmosphere did not cool off the earth as much as the Tambora clouds had, but the ash stayed there for three years before it settled. The dust made beautiful reddish sunsets all over the world during those years.

The most deadly volcanic eruption in the Western Hemisphere in modern times took place on the island of Martinique (mahrt-in-EEK), in the Caribbean Sea. On the northwestern end of the island is the volcanic Mount Pelée (puh-LAY). It hadn't caused much trouble in the past, but in April 1902 it began giving off smoke, ash, and fumes.

It didn't seem to get much worse, however, so people stayed in Saint Pierre (san-PYEHR), the capital of the island, which lay at the foot of Mount Pelée.

Somehow people got the idea that if lava did flow out of Mount Pelée, the shape of the mountain was such that it would not flow into Saint Pierre. For this reason people from the countryside actually came into the city for safety.

On May 7 there was an explosion not on Mount Pelée, but on Mount Soufrière (soo-free-EHR). This was a volcano on the island of Saint Vincent, one hundred miles south of Martinique. The Mount Soufrière eruption killed about two thousand people.

THE ERUPTION OF MT. PELÉE

On Martinique people couldn't help but feel relieved. They felt that whatever pressures were disturbing Mount Pelée were partially taken away by the eruption of Mount Soufrière. It seemed that Mount Pelée would become quiet now, and more people came into Saint Pierre.

Mount Pelée fooled everyone. At 7:50 A.M. on May 8, 1902, less than twenty-four hours after the eruption of Mount Soufrière, Mount Pelée exploded, too. A stream of lava slowly poured down the side of the mountain.

The people in Saint Pierre did escape the lava, but the explosion also produced a thick cloud of red-hot gases and fumes. These gases poured down the side of the mountain very quickly and headed straight for Saint Pierre. In three minutes thirty eight thousand people in the city were dead, having been burnt and poisoned by the fumes.

Not a single person in the city survived except for a criminal who was in an underground prison, and he just barely survived. He was supposed to have been hanged that very day, but he lived and everybody else died.

As far as American territory is concerned, there are volcanoes in Hawaii and Alaska.

The island of Hawaii, nearly as large as Connecticut, is all one huge mountain, the largest mountain in the world, though not the highest. Its highest peak is Mauna Loa (MAW-nuh-LOH-uh), which is over two and a half miles high—the tallest active volcano in the world.

On the eastern slope of Mauna Loa is a crater

ST. PIERRE AFTER THE MT. PELÉE ERUPTION

named Kilauea (KEE-low-AY-uh). It is two miles wide, the largest active crater in the world. It is always more or less active and lava occasionally runs over the top, but it doesn't explode.

TWO KINDS OF VOLCANOES

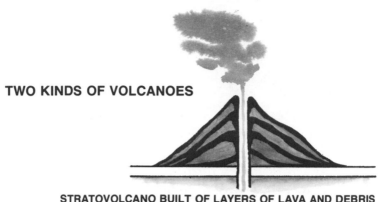

STRATOVOLCANO BUILT OF LAYERS OF LAVA AND DEBRIS

SHIELD VOLCANO IN MAUNA LOA BUILT OF LAYERS OF LAVA

The largest eruption in American territory in modern times came in June 1912, when Mount Katmai (kat-MIGH) in southern Alaska exploded. Five thousand square miles surrounding the volcano were covered with ash and dust, some of it reaching the city of Kodiak, one hundred miles to the east. The city was evacuated, but, on the whole, there were so few people in that part of Alaska at that time that little real damage was done.

In the forty eight states outside Hawaii and Alaska there is almost no volcanic activity. The only active volcanoes are in the Cascade mountain range, running north and south through the states of Oregon and Washington.

Fifteen of the peaks of the Cascades are volcanoes, though they have not been very active in recent years.

The highest peak of the Cascade Range is Mount Rainier (ruh-NEER), fifty miles southeast of the city of Tacoma, Washington. It is two and three quarters miles high, and though it is a volcano, it hasn't erupted in at least two thousand years.

A hundred miles south of Mount Rainier is Mount Hood, two and an eighth miles high, the tallest mountain peak in the state of Oregon. It, too, is volcanic, but it, too, has shown no signs of activity for a long time. By 1975, in fact, none of the peaks of the Cascade Range had shown any activity for sixty years.

About 135 miles north of Mount Rainier, however, is Mount Baker, which is near the Canadian border and is just two miles high. In March 1975 white smoke appeared over the mountain. People first thought that it was a forest fire, but closer examination showed that ash and fumes were issuing from its crater.

Nothing much happened to Mount Baker after that, but there was similar activity in Mount Saint Helens in southwestern Washington, just forty five miles northeast of Portland, Oregon.

Mount Saint Helens, which is not quite two miles high, had experienced considerable activity between 1831 and 1854. Not many people lived in the area at that time, so there were no detailed

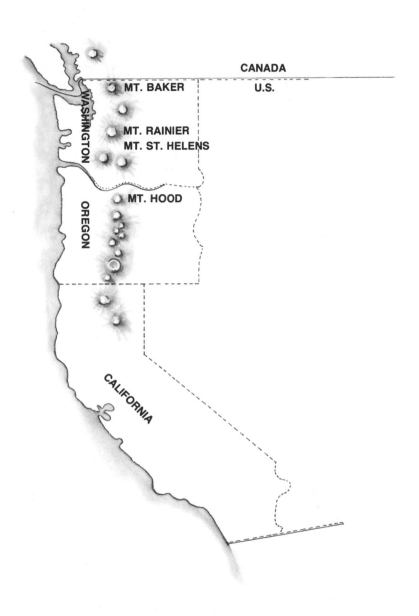

CANADA

U.S.

WASHINGTON

MT. BAKER

MT. RAINIER
MT. ST. HELENS

OREGON

MT. HOOD

CALIFORNIA

VOLCANIC PEAKS IN THE CASCADE RANGE

accounts of what happened, and not much damage had been done.

Mount Saint Helens, after 1854, remained quiet for a century and a quarter. It was a beautiful, snow-covered mountain and it was not thought to be dangerous.

But then, in March 1980, the region around Mount Saint Helens began to quake. There were frequent small earthquakes, and on March 27 some steam and ash were expelled by the mountain.

For about six more weeks, nothing much seemed to happen, and it seemed the activity would die away, as it had at Mount Baker in 1975. But then, on the morning of May 18, 1980, there were two stronger earthquakes and Mount Saint Helens exploded. It wasn't an enormous explosion of the Krakatoa type, but it was the largest seen in the forty eight states in all of American history.

Millions of tons of ash and rock were sent up as high as twelve miles into the air. Ash and dust sifted down for five hundred miles east of the volcano, in some places producing drifts three to four feet high.

The snow on Mount Saint Helens was melted and mixed with soil and earth to produce mudslides that swept away houses, automobiles, and bridges. Fortunately, most people in the area had left during the two months in which the volcano had been quaking and rumbling. Even so, more than twenty people were killed and over one hundred were reported missing.

BEFORE AFTER

THE ERUPTION OF MT. ST. HELENS MAY 18, 1980

What's more, Mount Saint Helens continues to erupt, and there's a chance that its present activity might continue for years.

There can even be volcanic eruptions in places where there is no mountain at all.

In Mexico, two hundred miles west of Mexico City, there was once a village named Parícutin (puh-REE-kuh-TEEN). On February 20, 1943, farmers were working in a cornfield three miles from the village, a cornfield that was perfectly flat. At 4 P.M. they noticed a crack in the ground. The crack began to widen. The ground quaked beneath their feet and flames and smoke began to shoot upward out of the crack.

The farmers left in a hurry and went back to their homes in the village. By next morning, there was a pile of ashes, one hundred feet high, over what had been a cornfield. More ashes and fumes kept coming out of the pile and it kept growing higher. It was a volcano that was growing larger and larger and came to be called Mount Parícutin.

By the end of the first year the volcano was fifteen hundred feet high and had spread out to cover the village of Parícutin, which was buried just as Pompeii had been but more slowly and without loss of life. By the end of the second year Mount Parícutin had covered a second, larger village, again slowly enough to allow its people to escape.

Finally, the eruption stopped in 1952, nine years after it had begun. By that time, Mount Parícutin was one and a quarter-miles high, and vegetation had been killed off for seven miles in all directions.

PARICUTÍN
A FEW MONTHS OLD

DAY

NIGHT

TOWN BURIED BY PARICUTÍN ERUPTION

TWO MILES DOWN IN AN AFRICAN GOLD MINE

4 The Heat Below Our Feet

WITH ALL OUR experience with volcanoes, do we know what causes them?

Yes, the old theory that there is a great deal of heat under the crust of the earth is still the only way to explain volcanoes. What's more, since ancient times we have come to know that there is heat down there because we can actually feel it.

In different places on the earth there are deep mines which are dug for gold, or diamonds, or other valuable metals and gems. The deeper the mine, the warmer it gets, and this is true no matter where on earth the mine is located.

The deepest mine in the world is in South Africa. It is over two miles deep and the rock walls of the mine at that depth are 126° Fahrenheit. People can't work in such deep mines unless cool air is pumped down into them.

Scientists are quite sure that the earth continues to grow hotter and hotter as the depth increases. At a depth of one hundred miles under the surface the temperature of the rocks is likely to be 2,000° Fahrenheit. On the surface, rock that hot would have melted into lava, but the rock doesn't actually melt because the pressure of the miles of rock over it weighs down upon it, squeezes it tightly together, and keeps it solid.

This layer of red-hot rock under the earth's crust is called the *mantle*.

About eighteen hundred miles under the earth's crust, the rocky mantle ends. Below it is the earth's *core*, which may be made up chiefly of iron and which is so hot that it is melted to a white-hot liquid. At the very center of the earth, the temperature may be as high as 5,000° or 6,000° Fahrenheit, and that is just about as hot as the surface of the sun.

There is plenty of heat under the earth to explain volcanoes, but where does that heat come from?

The answer depends on how the earth came into being. About fifty years ago many astronomers thought that the earth was originally part of the sun. They thought that along with the other planets, the earth had been torn out of the sun by the gravitational pull of another star that had happened to pass close by.

If that were the case, it wouldn't be at all surprising that the core of the earth was as hot as the surface of the sun. Fortunately, the outside of the earth cooled off to pleasant temperatures so that we, and all other kinds of life, can live on it.

However, the thought that earth was once part of the sun didn't hold up when astronomers looked more closely at it. There were flaws in the notion, and astronomers finally decided that the earth was never part of the sun.

In 1944 a German astronomer, Carl Friedrich von Weizsäcker (fun-VITES-sek-er, 1912–), returned to an older theory that had been thought wrong. He corrected some of its details and improved others until astronomers came to accept it.

According to this improved theory, the sun and all the planets were formed at the same time out of a huge cloud of dust and gas. The particles of dust and gas came together to form bigger particles, then still bigger pieces, and bigger ones yet. Finally large pieces of matter came banging together, pulled by gravity, to form worlds.

Most of the pieces of matter were at the center of the cloud, and they came together to form the sun, which is much bigger than all the planets put together. However, there was enough left over along the edges of the cloud to form the planets.

All the pieces that came together were cold, however. How did earth come to be so hot, then?

Well, when two pieces smash together under the pull of gravity, the energy of their motion turns into heat. As more and more pieces collide to form a larger and larger body, more and more heat is formed. Finally, by the time all the pieces have come together to form a body as large as the earth, enough heat has been released to turn the new planet white-hot.

Naturally, the more pieces that come together, the hotter the world. The planet, Jupiter, which is much larger than earth, is also much hotter in its interior. The sun, which is largest of all, is also hottest of all.

If the earth was hot to begin with, but has existed long enough for the outside to cool down,

FORMATION OF THE SOLAR SYSTEM

why hasn't the inside cooled down also? Why isn't the earth cool through and through?

The answer is that it takes a long time for heat to work its way through rock. Rock is an "insulator" that keeps heat from escaping. The cool rock on earth's surface is a blanket that keeps the layers beneath warm.

Still, even though heat escapes through the rocks of the crust very slowly, it does escape. After enough time the earth will surely be cool all through.

Back in 1900 most scientists thought the earth might not be more than 200 million or so years old, and that was not enough time for cooling through and through.

In 1905, however, an American scientist, Bertram B. Boltwood (1870–1927) showed how to measure the age of the rocks by the way a metal named uranium broke down very slowly to lead. This breakdown is called *radioactivity*.*

If a certain rock contains a small amount of uranium and a small amount of lead, both can be measured. Scientists could calculate how long it would take that much uranium to produce that much lead and that would tell them the age of the rock.

In this way, it was soon shown that the earth was several billion years old. Eventually, scientists were quite certain it was over 4 billion years old, more than twenty times as old as had been thought earlier. That makes earth so old that its interior should have had time to cool down quite a bit. That might mean there should no longer be enough heat underground to send volcanoes into great explosions—and yet volcanoes do erupt.

The answer lies again in the uranium. When

*See *How Did We Find Out About Nuclear Power?* (Walker, 1976)

bits of uranium turn into lead, a small amount of heat is produced. Uranium turns into lead so slowly, however, that we don't notice the tiny amount of heat produced by a pound of uranium, for instance. Still, if you calculate how much heat is produced by all the billions of tons of uranium in the whole world as it all slowly turns into lead, it turns out to be quite a bit.

Then, too, there are other substances that are radioactive, in addition to uranium. If all the heat produced by all the radioactive substances is added up, it turns out that the heat that is added to the mantle through radioactivity is about equal to the heat that leaks out through the earth's crust into outer space.

In other words, the earth is not cooling down at all. Radioactivity keeps the interior hot. Of course, little by little the uranium and other radioactive substances are disappearing as they turn into lead and other types of nonradioactive material. However, it would take many billions of years for the radioactive substances to dwindle to the point where the heat they produced would no longer be important. That means it will be billions of years before the earth will become too cool to have volcanoes.

But if the earth's interior is hot everywhere, why do volcanoes only appear in certain places on the earth?

It must be that the crust is not quite solid everywhere. There seem to be places where there are weak points in the crust; or cracks through which the heat from the mantle can work its way upward.

In some places, the heat gets close enough to the surface to heat up the water in the soil. That forms *hot springs*. Sometimes, the water is heated to the boiling point and then the steam that forms pushes the water above it high in the air, forming a *geyser* (GIGH-zer).

And, of course, if heat moves upward in large enough quantities, a volcano forms.

The weak spots in the earth's crust aren't just anywhere. Of the five hundred active volcanoes on earth, nearly three hundred are to be found in a big curve all around the borders of the Pacific Ocean, and about eighty more are along the Indonesian islands. This curve of volcanoes is sometimes called the *ring of fire*.

Scientists couldn't help but notice this in the 1800s. Some thought that perhaps the moon had once been part of the earth and when it had come loose it had left a hole that was filled by the Pacific Ocean. All around the rim of that ocean, they thought, were left the scars of that separation in the form of weak spots in the crust where volcanoes formed.

This turned out to be quite wrong. Scientists now think the moon was never part of the earth.

Suppose one marks off all the volcanoes on a map of the earth and adds the center of various earthquakes that have taken place. The ring of fire shows up and also other lines and curves on the map. The map of the earth seems to be divided into a series of large pieces, with volcanoes and earthquakes marking the edges.

Beginning in the 1950s scientists found much evidence to show that the crust of the earth actu-

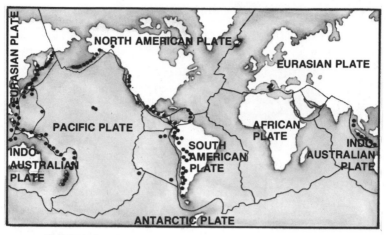

————PLATE BOUNDARY
• VOLCANO

TECTONIC PLATES AND THE "RING OF FIRE"

ally existed in the form of large plates which fitted tightly together.*

These plates slowly move. Although the rock in earth's mantle is solid, it is so hot that it can very slowly flow, like warm wax. Scientists think that there are slow circular currents of rock in the mantle. The currents, flowing across the bottom of the crust, drag the plates this way and that. Some plates are pulled slowly apart, some are pushed slowly together.

These motions set up weak points at the joints of the plates and through these the heat can flow upward to form volcanoes.

Can we predict when a volcano will become active?

Not yet, but perhaps, as we learn more and

*See *How Did We Find Out About Earthquakes?* (Walker, 1978)

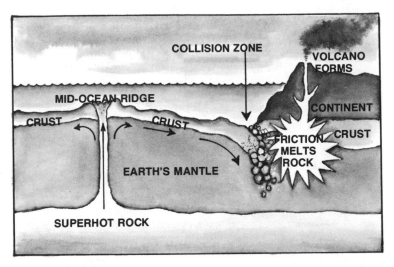

SEA FLOOR SPREADING AND FORMATION OF VOLCANO

more about the movement of the plates, we will find out how to make such predictions.

Can we find a way of preventing an eruption, or perhaps encouraging a small eruption before the pressures inside a volcano build up enough to cause a large one?

We certainly know of no way now, but there is no substitute for knowledge. Some answer may turn up as we learn more about the earth's crust.

CRATERS ON THE MOON

5 Volcanoes on Other Worlds

DO OTHER WORLDS have volcanoes?

It would seem logical to suppose so. When the solar system was first formed, the larger bodies in it must have been very hot. Once the outside began to cool down, there would have been large volcanic eruptions as the heat inside occasionally broke through the very thin, barely cool crust.

In some cases, though, the world may have been small enough to cool to the point where volcanic eruptions no longer took place. Or else, even if the inside of the world were still hot, the crust might have become too thick for the interior heat to find any weak spot through which it might escape.

There are places on the moon where you can see lava flows that cover thousands of square miles, but they all must have formed early in the moon's history. Right now there seems to be no sign of any volcanic activity at all.

In late 1971, a rocket probe, Mariner 9, was placed in orbit around Mars. It took photographs of Mars's surface, and from those photographs Mars was completely mapped.

There were craters, mountains, canyons, and other features on Mars. In one region, there was a series of large mountains with craters, and these were clearly volcanoes. The largest of these is now called Olympus Mons (oh-LIM-pus-MONS).

Olympus Mons is far larger than any volcano on earth. Its peak is about 15 miles above the average surface level of Mars, and its base is about 250 miles wide. It is twice as high as the volcano that makes up the island of Hawaii on Earth and three times as wide. What's more, the crater of Olympus Mons is 40 miles wide, much wider than the largest volcanic crater on earth.

As nearly as we can tell, however, Olympus Mons and the other Martian volcanoes are extinct. They have not erupted for a very long time.

In late 1978 a rocket probe named Pioneer

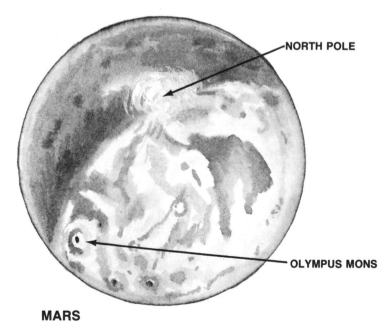

NORTH POLE

OLYMPUS MONS

MARS

Venus was placed in orbit about the planet Venus. The thick clouds that forever hang in Venus's atmosphere prevent the surface from being seen. Radar beams, however, penetrate the clouds and are reflected from the surface. By use of radar reflections, the instruments on Pioneer Venus mapped most of the surface of Venus.

Some of the mountains shown by radar seem to be volcanic. One possible volcano, named Rhea Mons (REE-uh-MONS), spreads its base over an area the size of New Mexico. If it is really volcanic, it is even larger than Olympus Mons on Mars. However, there are no signs of life in the volcanoes of Venus either.

There didn't seem to be active volcanoes anywhere in the solar system except on earth. But then, on March 5, 1979, a rocket probe, Voyager 1, flew past Jupiter and studied its satellites.

OLYMPUS MONS—EXTINCT VOLCANO ON MARS

There are four large satellites of Jupiter that are about the size of the moon or larger. The one that is closest to Jupiter is named Io (EYE-oh). It is just about the size of the moon and it is just about as far from Jupiter as the moon is from the earth.

The gravitational pull of Jupiter creates tides on its satellites. These tides squeeze and pull at the internal rock of the satellites and can act to heat them up. Io, being closest to Jupiter, gets more of the heating effect than any of the others do.

Just a few days before Voyager 1 passed Jupiter, some astronomers suggested that Jupiter's tidal action might make Io's interior hot enough to produce volcanoes. Then Voyager 1 passed Jupiter, took pictures of Io—and there were the volcanoes!

Eight volcanoes were detected on Io that were actually erupting. Four months later, Voyager 2, another rocket probe, passed, and six of those volcanoes were still erupting.

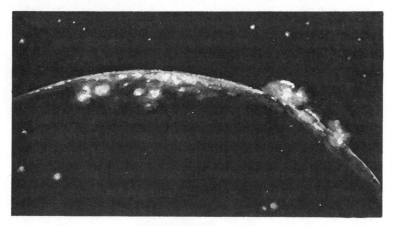

VOLCANOES ON IO

The volcanic eruptions on Io seem to consist largely of ash and of sulfur vapors. The whole surface of Io is colored red, orange, and yellow, thanks to a sulfur coating. There are also wisps of sulfur dioxide that forms a very thin atmosphere for the satellite.

So there are two worlds that we know about on which volcanoes actually erupt: Earth and Io.

Of course, it is earth's volcanoes that interest us more, for despite all our advances in science, our volcanoes are still killers and we are still helpless to do anything about them except run away when they erupt.

IO ORBITING JUPITER

Index

Alaska, 37, 39
Aristotle, 22
Athena, 22
Atlantis, 18

Baker, Mount, 40
Boltwood, Bertram B.,
    51
Brimstone, 26

Cascade Mountains, 39
Core, earth's, 48
Crater, 19
Crete, 9
    fall of, 16
Cyclades, 10

Earth, age of, 51
    origin of, 48
Enceladus, 22
Eruption, 14
Etna, Mount, 22, 30, 31

Geyser, 53
Gomorrah, 26
Greece, 16, 18

Hades, 25

Hawaii, 37
Heat, underground, 23,
    47
Hell, 25
Hephaestus, 20
Herculaneum, 28
Hood, Mount, 40
Hot springs, 53

Iceland, 32
Indonesia, 32
Io, volcanoes on, 60

Java, 32
Jupiter, 49, 59, 60

Katmai, Mount, 39
Kilauea, 38
Kodiak, 39
Krakatoa, Mount, 34

Laki, Mount, 32
Lava, 13
Lead, 52
Lipari Islands, 19
Lombok, 33

Mantle, earth's, 48

Mariner, 9, 57
Mars, volcanoes on, 57, 58
Martinique, 35
Mauna Loa, 37
Mexico, 44
Mines, 47
Moon, 53
  volcanoes on, 57
Moses, 21

Naples, 13, 27
New England, 34

Olympus Mons, 58
Oregon, 40

Pacific Ocean, 53
Paricutin, Mount, 44
Pelée, Mount, 35, 37
Pioneer Venus, 58, 59
Plates, crustal, 54
Plato, 18
Pliny, 28
Pliny the Younger, 28
Pompeii, 28
  ruins of, 29

Radioactivity, 51
Rainier, Mount, 40
Rhea Mons, 59
Ring of fire, 53
Romans, 19

Saint Helens, Mount, 40, 42
Saint Pierre, 35, 37

Saint Vincent, 35
Santorini, 11
Sheol, 25
Sicily, 19, 22
Sinai, Mount, 21
Sodom, 26
Sourfrière, Mount
South Africa
Strabo, 23
Sulfur dioxide, 26, 61
Sumatra, 34, 35
Sumbawa, 32
Sun, 48

Tacoma, 40
Tambora, Mount, 32, 33
Tartarus, 25
Thera, 11, 12
  explosion of, 16
Tsunami, 16

Uranium, 51, 52

Venus, volcanoes on, 59
Vesuvius, Mount, 27
Volcano, 21
  causes of, 22, 23, 53
  number of, 53
Voyager 1, 59, 60
Vulcan, 19
Vulcano, 19

Washington State, 40
Weizsäcker, Carl von, 49

Zeus, 22